copyright 2019 Jeanette Powers

cover design and logo by Elim J. Sidus

ISBN: 978-1-950380-67-1

LLOC: 2019953431

Spartan Press KCMO

@dandylion_riot

jeanettepowers.com

patreon.com/jeanettepowers

strange.gen.et@gmail.com

poems
by
jeanette powers

Table of Contents

Heart Clenches for the Grace of Folk	7
Dear Stranger	10
Dandylion Riot	12
The Red Doc Martins	13
The Hidden Letter: a painting by Kay Sage	15
Runaway with the Circus	16
Born Poor Stay Poor Rich in the Heart	18
Things I Imagine I Have in Common with Miley Cyrus	20
Jonah and the Whale	22
Things I Have in Common with Luke Skywalker	23
Don't Look Now Your Hands Have Grown Two Sizes	24
No Wonder	25
How We Move On	29
Cycles of Grief Go On and On	30
One and One is One	33
The Woodcutter	36
White Lies	39
Dogmeat (the fish)	40
The Vest	42
Hearts Break All the Time	44
Missing Pieces	45
The Mon Chi Chi	47
Sister, Sing Me	50
Steel Toe Boots Muse	51
An Elegy for Passing	52
Old Dogs	53
Dear God	55
Reeds in the Black River of Night	57

Don't Get too Close, I Guess	58
The War of Forgiveness	60
Paper Boats	62
A Friendly Gesture	63
Advice for Young People	64
The Bridge We Didn't Burn	65
I Know Who Would Win in a Fight	68
The Cost of Living	69
After Bouguereau's *The Bathers*	71
July 27, 1890	73
The Compass	78
You Were You When I Was Me	80
I Promised I Wouldn't Cut My Hair as Long as I Loved You	81
You Sing Your Arrows Against the Rock of Me	83
Still Singing, Now Dark	85
Dead Things I Excrete	86
Just Cause	88
Water is a Woman	91
Snippets of Poems that Didn't Make It into Poems	93

dedicated to the House of Flowers
who planted the seed of me
and grew me a new season

Heart Clenches for the Grace of Folk

It's the way everyone is walking around
with so much grace, knowing they are going to die.

There's a factory worker in Toledo
who turns off his heat in December
because work shut down for a week
and so he strikes the devil's bargain
of it's warm inside the apartment
or gas-station hamburgers and yard beer
it's how he saves all his aluminum empties
and puts them on the curb with a cardboard sign
that says *cans for redemption: return sign to porch*
and when he comes back from buying
another Natty Daddy to warm him in the night
the cans are gone and the sign
is propped up on his door.

There's an old man in a train station in Kansas City
who doesn't flinch at a four hour delay and says
we're waiting here or we're waiting somewhere else
and he and I dive into each other's lives
without wasting time on small talk
so we start on politics with religion
and within an eyeblink we're in real deep
about how my grandfather dying
left me all alone
and how his father dying
made him man of the house
when he was only ten years old
and how neither of us knew how to *do it*

how we had no one to show us the way
and I found solace in meth and squatting
and he found a crack pipe, inhaled deep
to fill in the gap of love the world took from both of us.

Of course, we agree.
We had to get our warmth
from somewhere and we all know
how that high makes everything else go away.

There's a single mother in Memphis
who announces she's pregnant again
on Thanksgiving Day over cornbread
when everybody knows she's already
stretched so thin she might break
but lift their glasses for a toast
to baby number four
to life's greatest blow against death
which is babies and being there for each other.

It's the immense generosity of the poor
that mends and patches and stitches
the elbow of your coat
the hand-me-down clothes
the wounds of everyday cruelties
a threat of the pipes freezing
missing another day with your mother
another lost week at a job you hate
another mouth to feed against the bleak
truth of less money and more winters
and more delays and the ever looming
certainty of death on the other side.

Every one of these everyday heroes
waiting on the inevitable as though it's *nothing*
penning another opening scene
never even mentioning the curtain call
worried in private but glowing
when you hold out a hand
all with the grace of folk
who warm you and mend you
and keep you from waiting alone.

Dear Stranger,

I very much enjoy a complete unknown.
To cast a net into the vast *everything is possible*
and come back caterwauling or enchanted.

I swim in murky waters
walk deer trails during new moons
when one can't even see the smallest
fingertip at arm's length.

You are a moon that needs a telescope
these letters are lenses we twist
and if I see your glowing surface
you also see the eye of my blue
peeping at you in wonder.

> *Who are you?*
> *Has anyone ever asked?*
> *What are your phases?*

There's something to a dark side never seen
a promise of an edge once stepped over
the moving of a body through the surface
of still water, a darkened foot
a detached hand.

A fish gasping in the air
pulled from a child's hands
and fileted by his grandmother.

What's within is its own unknown.

The wet and ancient interior
of its own infinity of stars
electric with memory
chance and even hope.

Hope is its own terror
the eggs of the shark
spilling on the butcher's block
a leech between your toes
a cave-in after you've passed
the deepest cavern.

We are trapped
with carbon water
lightless
cold

or maybe
with a full moon
a song, a soft bed and a shoulder
a place to rest your head.

Dandylion Riot

I am in the dark soil of winter
when you can see through
my canopy for miles
when I've lost all my leaves
and I'm hiding deep
when it's endless snow or 30 below
and the blank white of life is blinding
and we stop believing
we'll ever be warm again
I'm rootbound to this earth
when new moon and blackest night
when frozen mud chokes the earth
when all but hawks are hiding
I'm there, beneath the snow
pushing up through the ice
and one day in January
you will look down
and there
full yellow head
green shoot, tiny
dandelion
proving I never stopped
reaching for the sun.

The Red Doc Martins
    —for Morgan Thomas and Lori Sydney

I have worn many shoes
and I've thrown many shoes away
and I keep these because they hold
a bronze penny for you.

You told me about a fire in Iraq
that has burned continuously for over 4000 years.

Baba Gurgur, syllables of a babbling American infant
tyranny of a persistence, emanation of deep earth
this burning insistence, something out of our hands.

You told me you once tried
to keep a flame burning indefinitely
transferring its yellow red blue from candle to candle.

You only managed to keep it flickering for one and a half days.

I imagine standing in my oxblood Doc Martins
outside your window watching your ritual
flame as though it were an argument in your heart
about how much someone can make of commitment
or about how we can be a mirror to the world.

These shoes bind my feet and protect my ankles
the soles are thick and the laces are gold as incandescence.

I imagine your perpetual candle extinguished because
some errant breeze of a midnight open window

was the culprit: the wind is a worthy adversary
when it comes to games of persistence.

You said, *I imagine you'd be skilled at such things.*

I'm only standing outside everything arguing
with myself till I'm as old as Moses' tablets
standing on a penny, waiting for you to need good luck.

I imagine you looking at the snuffed flame saying

> *I'd rather have those boots.*
> *A good pair of boots*
> *will last forever.*

The Hidden Letter, a painting by Kay Sage
    —for Nadia Wolnisty

Once I painted a painting oddly similar to this one. It was a bodily form, but really it was the letter *i*, because I was afraid to be myself in those old days. At least afraid to be my vulnerable self, however unafraid I was to be my raging self. This fellow "Spike" was convinced we were soul mates. I was not. We were in his studio apartment, the shower was on very hot because that was how he heated his room. There was steam but it was all still cold. You could see your breath and the steam. He was very pushy. I said: *if you can tell me what this painting is really about, I'll agree with you that we are soul mates.*

Of course, he could not. I couldn't really either, beyond this knowing of a first "i". He struggled and grasped and kept insisting on another guess. We were on his bed which was a futon mattress on the floor. I kept standing up to leave and he kept pulling me back to the bed. I looked him in the eyes. I was silent. His face transformed. An iron plate appeared over his mouth. I remember there were rivets which closed his lips. He emanated the worst lime green sludge.

I felt sorry for him and left forever. Sometimes I see him walking alone on the streets around Gillham Park. Sometimes I'm walking alone, too.

Runaway with the Circus
        —for Michael Morales

Dream a but is life ...

We drank merlot from the bottle
in front of the bookstore
while he guessed the name
of my dead father
from the way
my eyelids twitched
while he said the alphabet.

I sang him *row row row your boat*
backwards while we stumbled
up 39th Street to his apartment
and climbed the ivy trellis
onto the back porch
because both of us enjoy
doing things the hard way.

He ran away to the circus
when he was 17 years old
and never went home again
made himself a mentalist
and goat whisperer.

Merrily merrily merrily merrily ...

That night
I took off my shirt
and without hesitation

laid down on his bed
of nails
he hollered *noooooo!*
but something inside of me
knew exactly how to do it
without ever being told.
Once you decide to commit
do it with your whole being
don't hesitate or take a small bite
move softly and breathe calmly

Stream the down gently ...

distribute your weight evenly
and then
enjoy
the thousand points
they feel like kisses

Boat you row row row.

Born Poor Stay Poor Rich in the Heart

Playing Monopoly
but backwards
where everyone
starts out broke
but when top hat lands
on the Electric Company
he gets a crisp peach 100 dollar bill
when rearing horse lands on Baltic Avenue
they get the purple card and 60 bucks

round and round
the board
drinking orange koolaide
with half the sugar
it goes down with chocolate chips
from the cookie baking stash
we add another limb from the back yard
to the wood stove in the living room
wrap in Grandma's corduroy quilt
hand stitched
and stitched again

Dad wipes the baby's nose
with a loose end of the thinnest strip
and everyone who passes go
gets 200 dollars
no one gets railroaded
or pays luxury taxes
and no one goes to jail
for not having enough

good rolls of the dice
we're only spending time
on top of the world
going round and round
and of course there's a winner

it's just whoever breaks the bank first.

Things I Imagine I Have in Common with Miley Cyrus

The things no one knows
about her are the things
she keeps closest to her chest
they are ornaments of equations
and capital T theories
they shimmer on the tree of her heart
and chime when the cat climbs high in the pine
she is not blonde in the math
of her private places
her tongue only sticks out
to lick stamps there
on the letter of her laws
she is not on stage
but at the desk of her secret mind
and there she finds all the graphs
and calculations that lead to answers
deep within Miley Cyrus
is an urge to know why
the diamond began as coal
to know how one proton
separates lead from gold
and it's important to know
her head spins with orbiting planets
it's important no one sees
the experiment her hands compose
figuring how long till the moon drifts away
it's important because if anyone knew
the grand universal longing of her alchemy
her need to be a changeling
her wish to rocket ship away

they would know
the things she doesn't want
anyone to know
she would become
a public figure
all the way through.

Jonah and the Whale

Did it begin with the creeping howl of wind in deep sea
hull creaking and sailor sick with the squall of the tempest
tempestual, unnatural?

Did it begin when He of the Uncaused Cause created himself
all powerful but still somehow prone, enjoying to toy with me
and command me to clean up after Him?

Did it begin with God's demand to send only me to that far off den
of iniquities with the gall of His condemnation on my lips
His words, my pointing finger?

Did it begin when I rejected divine decree and instead
boarded a ship of men God would see killed, if only
to punish me?

Did it begin when my lot cast me overboard into raging gale
a suicide over the ship's bow better than a sacrificed deck hand
and another widow, another orphan?

Who cares if that city of sin does burn in hell, let it be on God's heart
not by my hand. Windswept, sea-sick, I leapt into the mouth of that fi
like it was my salvation.

Things I Have in Common with Luke Skywalker

my parents are lost
I have a secret sister

we both know
that when shit gets cold
you have to kill your darlings
and live inside their guts

Don't Look Now Your Hands Have Grown Two Sizes
They look like good strong hands.
—Rockbiter, *Neverending Story*

How do you hide two houses behind your back?
I shake and shank the trembling does not
obscure how blown apart they rest in unrest
palms hover against my spine tight signing
ten thousand word essays
on stories I don't want to can't tell
how can this ramshackle keep coming up
plastic daisies as though they are my name tag

this left wrist was only a guest house
    she never said that
    I never left that way
taking the roof shingles
and wearing them as a corsage of thorns

my right hand gets caught up in the storm
all their detritus clinging like rat teeth to bones
this flesh flies and makes all my high winds
a shrapnel of fingertips and knuckles
everything I touch a demolition of crass
an emergency of the interior
no one declares me lost
but I'm gone
at the end of my arms

    I just want minuscule hands
    hiding in dainty lace gloves
    to bat long eyelashes
    and be loved.

No Wonder

When the girl arrived all blonde and blue
cutely confused, dearly innocent, plausibly harmless
and custom tailored with sailor dress and matching bows
she had that wide-eyed vulnerability only the truly
entitled and unharmed can ever dream to display.

Of course all the animals rushed to be near her
they and she both being so curious about her.
Some came with sheep's clothing, some came as real sheep
but all came *baaa-ing* and bowing to cater to her needs.
Who wouldn't want to feed her, drink her, grow her
and show her the lay of the land, go out of their way
to take her pristine, porcelain hand
and pay her unending praise?

I shook my head, watching her natural force
as she broke homes with her growing ego
writing-desks and heirlooms and plumbing and kitchens
all washed away in the tide of tears she wept
over how she herself had torn everything down.

What a lovely tautology, little Miss Liddell
answers her own questions, weeps over her own tantrums
and all the broken folks race to comfort and coddle her
without ever stopping to ask why.

I'm not as dumb as I look, you might not know
although I'm clearly mad, because I'm here.
I like poetry; and I know which road leads out of the woods.
I'm quite unlike that moonfaced brother of mine

his rotten cantaloupe head full
of wet tea-bags and dregs of wine
but us being twins, and him
ever in my care and tow
got me pigeon-holed by all the dodos
as just another half-wit thick-headed dope.
Which isn't the worst presumption since when people
think you are completely without gumption
they begin to think of you as nothing more
than absurdly moving furniture
and they will say just the most
barbaric things in easy earshot.

They assume a blank face is a safe face.
Why is precisely why I see all the angles in this house of cards.

So I laugh, as the daft do, because I recognize this imposing girl.
Me, dumb Tweedledum, can name this trespassing child:
she is merely *Alice of Wonderland*.

Even I saw her royal predecessor do the same:
take the throne from rabbit-hole to croquet ground
the inbred horror-show of power gone mad
someone who must be forever
the center of attention, however irrational
a little bully who holds their own ladder
who grows from blonde and blue and plausibly harmless
to painting the roses red and off with their heads
as quick as that rabbit who's late for a very important date.

O, I know the signs of an incipient tyrant:
she insists the scaredy unhoused Mouse think
arrestingly about Officer Cheshire Cat

who's always watching and always laughing
and always telling you how to act
whose bared teeth never quite fade
away with their permanent grin
from always having the upper hand.

She doesn't know where she's going
or care where she's been.

And so all of Wonderland bumbles and fumbles
and never grows because our leaders
are Queens of Hearts and Princesses Alice
and none of their affluent pampered asses
have the slightest idea of what it means
to live on the flooded streets
and run from burning houses
because of the violent whims
of the upper classes.

So forgive me
if I eat my oysters
when they are fresh in my hand
if I ignore the royal blonde heir apparent
and all her tried and true and blue bowed ideas
of how we shouldn't talk about yesterday
because she was a different person then.

Forgive me
if I don't think she has the right to grow
at such a rapid pace and I don't think
she should take up all the air.

Forgive me

if my daydream on the bank
is that me and Tweedledee
keep our cloak of invisibility
and one day
when no one
sees us coming
we take off
all their pretty heads.

How We Move On
—for Jeremiah Walton

Baby Bear is a dirty kid who uses my backyard firepit
to burn his journals in a Ceremony of Passage

we haven't invented new mythologies for centuries
and they become my first Vestal Virgin, a living altar

to the Nows of Travel and Homecoming and How
To Let Things Go That Once Were a Story Made of Iron.

How do we change the way we worship and murder?
Who can bid me arise from the Mist without chains?

There's an empty leash on the porch tied to a hand-woven rope
that used to keep my dog from running off into the wild.

Their pages float, charring up into the wind and are caught
on thermals, youth glows then turns to ash.

I watch from the kitchen window, still covered in frost
along the edges, I grow colder with distance.

I try not to think of my inner child dying with that dog
I invent that his death doesn't kill my longing to play and be loyal.

Baby Bear adds another book to the fire, it falls open
and the edges of the paper burn to the center.

Cycles of Grief Go On and On

In no good world is it right
for a mother to leave behind
two young boys when she dies
or for the family to fight
over her crumbs, her car
the paint by number of a white horse
the hand-painted sculpture
of a monkey, hanging from a real rope
the raining oil lamp
with the naked woman inside
there's no justice
in fighting over her wedding ring
while those two boys sit in pews
praying for their mom.

There is no kindness in giving
your queer granddaughter
a bible for graduation
after fifteen years of her
hiding behind the pulpit
knowing she can't be baptized
into the faith of her family
and cutting off her college fund
when she's caught red-handed
with a woman at the movie theater
then sending her out into the world
without a safety net
unable to pray without
remembering being cast away.

For the abandoned
it feels like everyone
has been beating on them
for their whole lives
and they are the only ones
paying the price
it seems like everyone is just getting away
with so much cruelty dressed up
as The Christian Thing To Do
and we, orphaned through grief
loss, through being different
we ritualize our own solace
and too often in razor blades
another dozen bottles of whiskey
always bashing our heads
in prayer against a wailing wall.

Are we raising a generation
of hungry ghosts, sleeping
with clenched fists?
Ready to punch back full strength
at first waking, every reason
heard as just an excuse
to keep us at arm's length
eventually unable to be given
an apology we can even hear
all we strays
always believing everyone
is going to be right at our throats
the second we show our true self
our rage is an impacted tooth
our memory an unfading bruise
the only cheek turned

always our own
and our knees worn to the bone
from unanswered prayers
always whispered alone.

One and One is One

Inside there was a tickle
it came from no one
and I laughed to myself
and gave chase but also I hid
because laughing alone
is for nutcases and criminal masterminds
the tickle became a tingle
I indulged because it felt so good
to leap off the high dive in second grade
when the other girls all said *no way*
and it felt mighty to tell a tall tale
better than the boys on the playground
and the tingle was more discreet
than the tickle because goosebumps
are quieter than a giggle but that's part
of how I learned to be quieter, too.

More than one grown up said to me
    you're different
and some said it with a sneer
but a few said it with pride
and I admit I liked being on the outside
so I chased that tingle till it was a tug.

And the tug whispered in my ear
if you can dream it, you can be it
and for whatever reason I believed that
while also knowing to keep it a secret
so I shushed that part of me that was different
enough to get good grades, get a good job

and all the while that tingle inside
kept me laughing and kept tugging
and kept expanding like a helium balloon
filled with carbonation until I liked
the secret world better that I liked the real one.
Then out of nowhere the tug became a tumble
I'm picking myself up off the ground
everywhere I go and the tickle is escaping
because I can't stop saying *we're not apart*
we are a part and inside is this infinity
and outside the powers-that-be are trying
to separate into one or the other
into with us or against us, into rich or poor
black or white, elephant or ass, masculine
or feminine as if any of this night and day
was without twilight or sunrise, as if it wasn't
all one earth and sun and spinning
and the dance of planets and the lucky chance
that we are all here and we are all one.

We are not bound by the shape of our body
we are not constructed of what society invented
we are luminous beings made of star dust
who are free to choose how we grow in the world
and what is clear as the day is long
is that every separation is an act of division.

So call me non-binary, philosophically
politically and in this person
I am not one or the other of anything
I'm tickled and tingled and tugging
because I sensed from the beginning
that what was different about me

was believing there was no difference
so great between boy and girl
teacher and student, self and universe
this moment and the whole spectrum
that any of us could really be separate
from our heartstrings, our experience.

We are not either a zero or a one
we cannot be reduced to opposing natures
we are the universe looking at itself
and not just saying *anything is possible*
it's saying *everything, everything, everything.*

The Woodcutter
> *Children, especially young lasses, pretty, courteous and well-bred, do very wrong to listen to strangers.*
> —Charles Perrault

Wolfie and I's little game surely never did anyone any harm
we prowled the edges of the meadow so discreetly
learned the routines of the men who cleared the woods
and the villagers who delivered goods from town to town
the day trip days of hermit types who lived deep in the forest.

Truth be told, Wolfie was shy, even a little self-loathing
being so long in the fang, muzzle dusted gray, and coat patchy
and it pained him to watch his wild home be torn down day by day
by his own sweet woodcutter, lumberjack lover … me.

He wasn't the first victim to find his perpetrator arousing.

Hers wasn't the first riding hood, either.
Old Wolfie had been at all the ladies' clothes lines for years.
A ruffled bonnet here, granny panties everywhere
once a traveler sent a silk negligée out to wash, well …
let's just say neither of our appetites could be whetted.

He felt so complete in those lady clothes, and me?
I felt like a King with hands clenched round
wolf's strong hips where I became master
of man and beast alike.

Really, I and he both should've known
the whole ruse was too good to last
but that Old Bitty's boondocks house

was the ideal venue for our illicit rendezvous.

Old girl and the whole damn town went to church
every Sunday till afternoon, giving us that most remote home
all to our greedy, gluttonous, gorgeous selves.

It's fair to say we got comfortable in our arrangement
didn't notice Grandmother had gone elsewhere that day
didn't consider that someone might come merrily by
in bright cloak with bread and honey checking up after her
we never imagined what would happen if
Little Red Riding Hood would happen upon …

> *what big strong arms to hold me with*
> *what darling long, soft big ears to whisper into*
> *what big wet wanting eyes to gaze upon*
> *what big dangerous and sweetly nipping teeth he had!*
> *O, to so sweetly bite me with …*

I grow nostalgic.
I miss him most days, you know.
Can't help remembering back to that fateful day
and how I sold my innocent Wolfie to an early grave.

He was warmly sleeping
all dressed up in Grannie's clothes
waiting for me to creep in under the bobbin and latch
sneak under the covers to grasp and kiss and spread
and lick and suck and pound my dearest, darling howling pet.

While he daintily snoozed, sawing all those dreamy logs
Red did bring her get-well cake, her little butter pot
laying down her riding cloak and then herself in feather bed

next to what she so wrongly thought
was her sick with fever, sleeping Grandmama.

A shame I didn't notice her there
but instead went straight away at pleasuring my Wolfie.

Such a bad dog, playing that waiting teasing game with me
lacey and frothing in that old bat's goose down bed.
I did bend over my Wolf in Grandma's Clothing
with such raw relish and I did push my axe in deep
and how we howled together in forbidden ecstasy.

Which of course is what woke Red up.

Which is what Red awoke to.

Of course I had to act fast
grabbing my other axe I slashed
and the hot spurting spray of my lover's artery burst
and splattered against the quilted bed, our little Red
the bloodshed stains the floors to this very day
and Wolfie went down in a way that didn't please me at all.

In the confusion of the aftermath, I spun a tall tale:
telling Red how lucky she was I'd come along
at just the moment he was about to eat her whole
and saved her innocence from that Big Bad Wolf.

I mean
what would the townspeople think
if they found out about my wolfish delights?

> Better to put him down
> than be found out.

White Lies

There's a special kind
of cruelty
to saying certain things
without meaning it:

> *I'll be home soon.*
> *I love you.*
> *I'm sorry.*

Dogmeat (the fish)
      —for Isaiah Devine

I recognize this boy
ten, maybe eleven years old
in the pool hall begging games off the men
who will all teach him a thing or two
about cues, shots and scratches.

This is the same long hair and tight shoes boy
I met at the town fair on a Friday night
where I was working the ticket booth
with the bank ladies and retired vets
and this boy comes up to me all smiles
with cotton candy in one hand
and a tiny white and orange goldfish in the other
won from one of the ring toss fair games.

This fish is dogmeat for sure
it'll never survive the tilt-o-whirl, the ferris wheel
I mean it's got like two hours of air in that plastic sleeve
he pushes the fish into my line of sight
he's got me pegged as the bleeding heart all right
and says: *Hey, do you want this fish?*

Every part of my being says *absolutely not*
except for my mouth, which blurts out *sure*
because this boy and me and that fish
have one thing in common
we all know what it's like to not have a shot.

The kid runs off with his friend to the next ride

and I get off my shift and drive to the 24-hour superstore
and get a tank and food and a bubbler and water ph toner
laughing with Nathanael about how much it takes
to keep a measly goldfish alive
and my friend names him "Dogmeat"
because we're still not sure he'll survive.
Now, months later
drinking whiskey at Padgett's Pool Hall
in this small town nowhere Missouri
this kid comes right up to me
asks: *how's the fish doing?*

Fine. Growing big and strong.
I say, and it's true.

The kid runs back to the pool table
he's biting his tongue and holding up
the too-heavy cue stick, one eye on the ball.

We're both counting on him making it.

The Vest

Cream nearly corduroy
an unidentifiable, soft fabric
16" across at the arm pit
there is a sweat stain
tea leaves whispering
14.5" across the waist
my father was a thin man

there's nothing in the two front pockets
not hand made, but also not store bought
every stitch holds its place
no button has frayed its setting
they are not buttons, they are snaps
copper and marked by nautical stars
it's said everyone was starstruck by him

I imagine his skinny and bronzed arms
slipping into the vest, over silk butterfly collar
and mahogany bellbottoms
maybe from when he had a perm
and that '70's faux-fro
or when he was younger
and mousy brown shoulder length
covered his eyes as he played bluegrass

I don't know how this vest came to me
or why I found a metal hanger and a plastic white rose
and paired them all together
but this arrangement
has been my altar to my father always

and is all I really have left of him

somedays, I lean in and smell the pit stain
press my face to the breast, I reach into the pockets
and conjure holding his hand.

Hearts Break All the Time

I remember the gnarled hands
of my grandfather working the rotary dial
of the old goldenrod yellow Ma Bell telephone
calling the hospital where my grandmother lay
waiting to have her chest cracked
for a double bypass
heartbreak was not new to her

I hung my fingertips
on the tall bureau with the phone
and the lazy susan with her fake pearls
watching him talk and listening
>*I love you, Helen*
I'd never heard him say that before
tears fell down through the stubble of his cheeks
they were the bluest eyes I've ever seen

his hand always trembled for a cigarette
and it did then too, they are decades gone now
just like land lines and my youth

the doctor is earnest
reading my genome results
tells me I can't absorb folic acid
or Vitamin D, my liver is weak
and that no matter how healthy I am
a future heart attack is certain

>*I've already survived several*
I assure her with a smile.

Missing Pieces

I don't own a single object
that belonged to my Aunt Zoe
there's nothing here to throw away or keep of hers

there is a crumpled yellow flyer
advertising her band *Zoe and the Mofoes*
they played basement jazz clubs in Kansas City
her fingers flying over keys and bawling heartmelt
chin lifted neck crooked eyes closed voice undaunted
against the pathology of buckle dropped against a child's floor
against the loss of a firstborn and a brother and still more
everything I have of hers she handed to me
with the breath of her survivor's song.

She was a glassblower, too
making unicorns and dragons spun with fire
in the living room while I read library books nearby
when a piece of red hot glass went flying off the bench
and quickness yes, did catch that old carpet right on fire
she yelled with brass balls and kind tyranny
    get water get water
so I run into the kitchen and all I can find
is a tiny yellow plastic butter dish we save
because we can't afford tupperware

I fill it up with sink water
and run it to the fire in the front room
it's splashing out everywhere, there's no water even left
I get right close to the growing flame
and dump five measly wet trickles, they do nothing
so Zoe jumps out from behind the glass blowing station

runs outside and gets the garden hose
brings it right into the house
and sprays the living room fire out of existence
saving the day
we just laughed and laughed
and sat on the smoky couch
with a burned-out front room
and she looked at me and says:

> *well, if it's not a rash on your ass it's a pimple on your pussy.*

I come across her unexpectedly
in a photo album my ex-husband
returned to me years after the divorce
because his version of asking forgiveness
is promising to never remember you ever existed
and there is Zoe, she's the mother I remember
in a white dress with Spanish embroideries
smiling bright red hair
and she's laughing away all the pain
and she's who taught me to giggle
cackle, crack knuckles, howl at the world
and there's no way to pack that into a moving box
although I've lost and found it more than once.

I light the advertisement on fire
and imagine letting it drift
dangerously close to the floor
cock my head and listen:

> piping up from a basement window
> in a back alley with echoes of laughter
> a lost blues diva sings a refrain
> about how you can't take nothing with you.

The Mon Chi Chi

Aunt Sonja died of diabetes
and having watched another aunt later
go this same way, I don't think anyone
really gave their best effort to stop her
or maybe everyone hates themselves
or knows they couldn't do any better
or maybe just no one knows
how to tell someone *I don't want you to die*
so we let them eat taffy and pineapple upside down cake
and look away at the endless pitchers of sweet tea
or another case of the cheapest beer
because we're all so poor anyway
what's one pleasure today?

   Easy for me to say.

So Sonja has two adopted sons, Chip and Dale
absolutely no fooling, but this is still a story
about a stuffed monkey, a Mon Chi Chi
me and her saw on TV and little we had
but I told her I really wanted one, anyway
and for whatever reason she gumptions up
gears up the grumbling Ford Pinto
and heads to Indian Springs Mall
in Wyandotte County, Kansas
and in the two of we go.

The first thing we see is Helzberg Diamonds
I've never seen so much glittering light
it's the whole star field a crazy planetarium

caught in a sea of taupe carpet and beige walls
and queerly above, my first ever chandelier
Sonja hands me down a bright red button
and pins it on my shirt, she tells me it says:

    I am loved.
I'm not even five years old
but it's easy to remember what it felt like
it felt like my first big announcement
I am loved and it was Sonja who loved me
and she scooped me up and wandered me
through the rest of the mall, my first mall
on the way to Children's Palace
the Holy Grail of a 1980's kid's life.

I remember her carrying me way more
than I remember picking the little monkey
out from all the other identical stuffed monkeys
but I'm sure I was glowing and I know
I was just over the moon in love with her
and looking back, the money she spent
was probably meant for insulin.

    We all live with what we owe.

Sonja and I went to Orange Julius
after getting my hot new toy of the season
and I set my brown paper bag under the bench
where we drank the frozen juice, powdered sugar
powdered egg, vanilla milk perfection of a slushy treat
and I was loved and winking at people passing by
and everyone was laughing and kind and happy
so we walked away with a gasp of joy in our hearts

that wasn't all that common in a family sick with silence.

I still have that useless monkey
and I still wonder what happened to Chip and Dale
after Sonja died, and wonder why not one
of the family has ever tried to find them
and I watch my cousin Sheri at the candy
and she is so sweet I can't even say
I don't want you to die.

> *They say diamonds are forever*
> *but that's a fucking lie.*

Sister, Sing Me
        —for Jessica Ayala

Sister, sing me the mountain song
of your ancestors who know
how the tear falls from the stone
and why the ocean heals our troubled hearts.

Who take the arrows from the quiver
transform them into lilies
and the nourishment of family.
The song is behind your ears

which carry light air of the Andes
deep sediment of kingfisher and toucan
your eyes speak the chiming breath
of a blessed kiss on the forehead.

Your ancestors trust you
with the secret names of planets
pulling you into the future
they know your strength when you do not.

You were sent to a foreign hemisphere
with your braids pleated panther sleek
with drumbeat rising in your tongue
and a language beyond the cliff and delta.

Yours is a song of salt and net and trill
you heave and sing under the weight of life
rich with sweat under the medicine feather
the peak of the summit is your gift to give.

Steel Toe Boots Muse
        —for Jason Ryberg

Long in the tooth and by that I mean
you talk up a Kansas duststorm
and short on the booze which means
you drank through Uncle Dwayne's moonshine
before sunset and now you are kickin clay dirt
and loose gravel walking the fire road
up to the cemetery and your boots are old, friend
used to be mahogany brown till the drought won
and burnished them right down to a god-only-knows
shade of this-shoe-walked-a-long-goddamn-way
and right there in the middle is a bald spot
shining bright silver steel saying
    I could kick a hole right through you
but it likely ain't gonna happen today
them boots are leather tough
know a tractor clutch and a jackhammer in the gut
and laid enough tile to pave I-70 to Denver and back
and those steel toes be found tapping to the radio
somewhere in the deep country
somewhere in the big city
running dirt roads with me
turning day dreams into tall tales
and no matter how well we harmonize
the song always goes, brother
the song always goes.

An Elegy for Passing

The day I found out
I had to put my dog to sleep

after we saw his spine deformed
under the weight of carrying his own weight
on two front feet alone
and watched him struggle
to sit for a treat, eyes dark with pain

his was agony but you were cruelty
with a litany of whining rage
you told me you don't have time for friends
while I was counting minutes
left with the best one I'd ever had

the tantrum of you boomed
that I need too much emotional support
I was all wet graveyard, mud and tears and ice
I asked: *is this because
I'm sad about the dog dying?*

*no, it's because of you
asking me to clean the sink*

you are just a shadow passing over this moment
where I hold my friend until his last breath
look him in the eye and tell him it's alright
where he and I know what it means
to be there for each other to the end.

Old Dogs

We are at a kitchen table
and sitting at opposite ends
it is not your table, or mine
there is a rotting lemon
dessicated ginger root
all things grow old.

This table doesn't get much use
outside of our meeting here
you cook up stories of Toledo
your grandfathers and death
I tell you about dandelions
and how I think of you
as the one we saw popping
from under the snow
the day we walked
to the cemetery.

Which is not our graveyard, either
but a borrowed valentine
with an old dog chasing a squirrel
he'll never catch again
since his knees gave out
and we both know something
about how the body
can't anymore.

We go out to eat yesterday
and today and don't talk about
tomorrow, ever

your right hand palsies still
both of mine are growing surely
into the shape of my grandmother's
in our eyes are tombstones
but we are holding fast
to what's left after the rest has gone.

Dear God,

I don't want to fuck you as the all-powerful creator
because I don't see you as immovable
I don't worship you as father
and I don't worship you as son
a fragile shard of human flesh, dying
on a crucifix of forgiving men for their sins
only to be whispered about at altars
in reverent awe and never to be crossed
without risk of unending damnation.

In my hands, you are man and blush and rough
and muscle, a being to kiss and touch
and take to the wreckage of my bed
which means we'll pain and throw
and grunt and get too close
to the razor wire skin of each other
and surrender, give in
to the holy consummation.

Dear God, I see everyone cower
and cling and pray at your feet
and I know you like it
always getting your way
and praise and halleluiah
they told you so often
that you can do no wrong
you began to believe it was true.

I'm your little wanton Devil
you love to make me small as snuffed candles

to tell your legions you will never let me into Heaven
but we both know you carry me close, closest even
if you didn't love me so irreverently
love my truth, my need, my seeing
you as mortal, touchable
then letting me in wouldn't murder you so.

Reeds in the Black River of Night

Whisper kisses
reeds in the black river of night
curled fist of seeds
against pale thigh sighing
my breath heaving
your throat moan
quiet as moonrise

arm over belly
fallen sycamore in the press
caught fingers under water
swell of hip so delicate
a landscape of permission
spoken in waves
like a native tongue

I pull against you
the rock of my heart caught
holding fast to the shoreline
your fingertips are rough edges
but your touch is silt and feather

I don't surrender
but I want to.

Don't Get too Close, I Guess

I would run my fingers a race
to the ribbon scar on your cheek
through your tangled hair
we would catch our own breath
and laugh nervously

but we believe we can't give in to risk
this easy way of what we've carefully built
or chance being seen closely
it's the peril of the starting gun
when we both know
how violent the secret side of us is
the side we're scared to share, I guess

you are sick and afraid you'll die
too soon and only break love's heart

what if a shoulder held
turns into a mingling of fingers
what if our need leans in
and we breathe each other's breath
but we would not hazard the press of lips
that can't be taken back, I guess

I am sick and afraid I'll rabbit run
as soon as love burrows in

so every time
I rest my head on your shoulder
the whisper between us says

    be serious
and we laugh nervously

and both of us are really terrified
that we are actually unlovable

I'm wishing we weren't so unwilling to find out, I guess.

The War of Forgiveness

I want to say I didn't burn your dinner
on purpose, the oven was broken, the timer
didn't work right, the radio distracted me
I know how much you love your biscuits
and how eating is when you are happy.

You push the plate away with a sneer
and so I eat the last bit of tough gizzard
because I can't bear to disappoint you
and I want to hide away my mess
like a dog eating its own vomit.

When I take the last black bit of meat
off your plate you greedily bite my tongue
so now I cannot say *I'm sorry*
because your teeth are in my mouth
which swells shut against your hunger.

Now you have to break every dish I've served
so I flip the table scatter the evidence and you
scramble over shards of cheap corningware
periwinkle patterned, a platter we inherited
from our parents, a chalice from their wedding.

My scream is muffled under your bleeding palm
lacerated on the broken casserole glass
and I can't help but suckle like a babe
because I will take the smallest nibble
I am always starving to death in your presence.

Our blood mingles at fingers, fist and tongue
your tears fall small seasonings into my eyes
this is the fullest we will ever be again
but we can't see through salt wreckage
or speak through broken teeth.

The fried chicken is smashed into the linoleum
and wasted across the checkered kitchen floor
when once the dishes were clean and dry
where once we drank sleepy time tea softly
and cleared the table and loved each other.

The worst of it is how we know we'll just
leave everything in this state of shambles
our mouths full of broken plates and grit
and grudges we'll savor like fine wine
famished in a world of otherwise plenty.

Paper Boats

The page wanted to be a novel
but couldn't even make a chapter
I folded it into a crane
as a way of saying *I'm sorry*

it couldn't fly
instead sat steady on the book I was reading
I unfolded the wings
and smoothed out the creases

the page wanted to be a plane
but it was already a two-dimensional rectangle
I folded it into a boat
and took it to the river

we've been through so much together
I've erased more than I've mentioned to you
now we are at the shore
and I set the soft over-folded paper into the current

watching it float downstream
there is a direct line to the page and my heart
the line is invisible
made both of hope and loss

I rise from the flat surface of water
the paper boat grows smaller and smaller.

A Friendly Gesture

The fence is covered in roses
and the rain is pooling
on the end of every needle
the pine tree owns

May decided to take
December back again
you know how they
make-up break-up

my winter coat doesn't mind
one last tryst for old times sake
I sit outside on the damp bench
and watch spring with myself alone

it's funny how we think
chain link really keeps people out
how walls seem to make us feel safe
as if we could barricade the world away

like love isn't walking through the gate
with a smile on their face
like love isn't the most dangerous thing
that could happen to you.

Advice for Young People

Take your shoes off and get a nice case of ringworm
then you'll know how to spot it and figure out how to cure it

then pick up a toad and let it pee down your wrists
so you'll learn first-hand you don't get warts and how soft he is

just for grins practice being still enough to catch a skink
without grabbing it by the tail which *will* fall right off

walk down the hill to the river on a new moon night alone
take off all your clothes and swim in the starry dark

don't leave the current because you are cold or tired
stay through to bright shiver, learn how not to get bored

stop believing everything you were told by adults
don't think they are lying, they just only know what they were taught

learn the difference between something you are told is fact
and something people have just been saying for a long time

don't tell everyone what you've learned
it's fun to believe in ghosts and monsters and god

if someone asks what you think, that's your shot
tell them everything you've learned from the toad piss.

The Bridge We Didn't Burn

I have a husband
he lives in Toledo
with his girlfriend
well, his ex-girlfriend
because they couldn't
figure this whole mess
out any better than we could.

He has a new friend or two
some are ladies and some are not
and he's in love with them and with me
and with Sugar Momma in LA
and if you met him
he'd probably be in love with you too.

He has that kind of heart.

The first time I went to his apartment
there was a layer of cigarette ash
a quarter inch thick on the floor
a sculpture of natty light cans
towering in the corner
a shopping cart and a museum
dedicated to the memorabilia
of his every past love.

He said:
> *they are my pantheon*
> *I will never stop loving them.*

It occurs to me that there's no example
of how to do the middle part of love.

Beginnings are all making out in public
and panther cuddling in matching Doc Martins
and falling asleep with his dick in my hand.
Endings are all breaking up in public
and metaphorically kicking each other's faces apart
and falling asleep in separate rooms alone and sad
in the house we never should have moved in to.

I decided on that first day with him
that I loved his loving all his exes so much
and maybe I rushed into being an ex, too
but here's the thing:
    I'm not.
I'm not an ex
because I let him keep loving me
just like he so desperately wants to
but in the wholly new way.

We never wanted to get rid of the love
only the fighting and the pain
and the kicking and the running
the impossible expectations
and the silent mouths, the deaf ears.

And now my husband and I
well ex-husband legally
we are inventing whole new middles
middles so wide it tasks
imaginary architects to figure out
how to span the distances.

We built the kind of home neither of us
knew before we knew each other
one we're never thrown out of
where we're never giving up on
where we're not just allowed
to be ourselves, but celebrated
adored, treasured even nurtured.

A place it's safe to say:
> *I'll be there for you no matter what.*

I Know Who Would Win in a Fight
       —for Daniel Crocker

Once I watched a tiny black cat take down a possum that lived in the basement of my house. She wanted the warm spot for the winter. The cat left the possum dead in the street. We let her stay and I named her Spare Cat. She had specks of white in her dark fur, like a starry night. When she was on the porch, she would sit on your lap; everywhere else, she was pure feral. She would hunt birds in the trees in our front yard and *parkour* all theatrically with murder on her mind. She never went hungry. She knew who her friends were.

The Cost of Living

This poem is for the men buried
in the Westinghouse Bridge
the one Pittsburgh takes
when things get serious
the one that looks over Braddock
and the valley of steel
where the men come home
covered in coal dust
from fingernails to lungs
and the fires burn day and night

where everyone knows there's
only one way in and one way out
and work until the day they are forced out
work until the end of their shift
then stop at the bar for a beer or two
where the bartender's singing
 I was made for love and booze, baby
while the wife and kids are waiting and hoping
 nothing happened at the plant today

the missus drives a car littered
with dead flowers and lotto tickets
from bouquets gifted from the mister
to keep her from worrying
and from her scratching luck every day
for the chance of getting him
out of the valley forge
to a place of no worries

but nobody's leaving
and everybody wields a prayer
for the men in the tomb overhead
called the Westinghouse Bridge
a prayer of hope and knowing
how the cost of living is rising
always rising.

After Bouguereau's The Bathers
        (italicized lines from the *Inner Chapters of the Tao*)

Don't forget how to listen
or if you have
drop everything and run
to a sandbar in a river
you'll probably have to swim

take off your shoes before you leave
take off your clothes before you get there

it will be chill and brisk
there will be fish who nibble
the round peach fuzz of your bare thighs
and toes and elsewhere, too
let them

be quiet
remember you know where you are
this is it
remember you know how to breathe

yes, fresh, yes
your body grows heavy
you stop holding yourself up so much
you put your mind in its own pocket

you are hear
you are here

lay on the sand and spread your legs

show the sun your whole body
there is no shame

the heron flies over you
the warbler continues her lunch
deep sip fresh water across the way
and a salamander rests near your foot

you are part of this
your body will always remember
but you will always have to remind your mind

> *happiness is light as a feather*
> *but none can bear it*
> *calamity is heavy as the earth*
> *yet none can avoid it*

there will be another storm
but right now
you stand naked
before everything there is
and all is right with the world.

July 27, 1890
> *What would life be if we had no courage to attempt anything?*
> —Vincent van Gogh

The man grips the sides of me
with two hands although I have no word
for the number two
(or word for hands)
or mouth by which
to speak what I understand
to be words among men.

This man does not speak, either.

I'm gripped and hefted
and accompanied by familiar things:
an arrangement of wooden sticks
some long and bound together
in an arrangement which allows them
to stand pyramid under cadmium yellow sky and sun;
some wooden sticks smaller and smoother
and bound at the tip with sable, or hog bristle
by a circle of pressed metal.

There is also a parcel of leather
with a hand-stitched strap which crosses
my man's heart and rests on his shoulder
and carries within many a different type
of vibrant which are encased in a very thin metal,
and when they are pressed, gently
(not gripped like me)
there emerges a substance, oily and bright

a substance which reflects a life of colors
each tube its own impossible hue.

This man, who carries me
has the power to combine them
such that he will make a mirror of me
(where he is the prism)
I will become the reflection
of how he sees the world.

On my back is a rectangle of wooden sticks
which make what he calls a frame
and tacked into my solid empty outline
is a lead white linen stretched taut as a skyline
at the horizon over the waving sea
and this is what becomes the front of me
what he and everyone one calls a *blank canvas.*

He clutches me under arm and over satchel
with easel in the other hand and traipsing
over root and past trunk and beyond the sunflowers
this man hurries us off to where we don't know
and won't have words for until he has given us title.

I know I will be named for what he refracts
onto me and not for what I am.

The sun is diminutive today and less interested
in land than in the tops of grey threatening clouds
this man relentlessly onwards through the underbrush
past the olive trees to where the number that is three
three paths intersect and we, blank canvas, wooden sticks
and leather satchel are all dropped to the ground.

He paces, his straw hat is nearly windblown away
his tongue licks his thumb, he cocks his head
and at once falls to his knees and I swear
    his body shuddered
his shoulders heaved and his
heavy potato-eating hands
winged to cover his face like a bible
as he sharply caught his breath.

(This is a moment of deep pause.)

He resurrects and his fingers run the edges
of his eyes, flicking, winging out to the side
as though taking flight.

He was a man who wasted no time
he set easel and satchel and breath in and out
and took paints and palette and brushes
and set me in the nest of the view
of a wheatfield
brassy, golden braided grain
topped with slender translucent feathers
small and thin in the wind, like him
this field, fertile, ready for the reaping
topped heavy with grain frenetic in the coming storm
he gripped me and lost the covering of his head
as the tumult of the breeze turned brazen.

This man of skin and bones who fed the stray dog
his last bit of bread though brother to a rich man
began his painting with angry strokes of cobalt blue
darkened and thick on his brush
he pressed color to the canvas impasto

his deep abyss, his chasm, his crevasse
he lay his dirt of canyons and loss, pure color
pure hue next to pure rue and this world
emerges, still: the brush taken to his tongue
the bristles wet with his spit
and the oil dripping in his beard, red
alizarin as his pumping blood.

His movement was a reflection of the movement
of impending squall, a mirror of heavy wheat
whipping itself against the inevitable
that makes he and the grain
and the image and the bread
and the heart and the belly
and the invisibility of the unseen
and the need to take some stand.

I felt the storm within him blow across the blank of me
and come to an eye as he filled me full
(as he would never be filled)
he poured himself into me
gave me everything he had
and knew and saw
while he starved
and wasted away
he starving in a field of plenty
he destroyed in a world of wealth.

And in the thunder of his wrist's last motion:

>	the black
>	black of crows
>	black of loss

black of must go
the black of crows
a murder of crows
a suicide of crow
dispersed in all directions
startled heavenward
by a single
shot.

The storm spits
and the man falls.

A single drop
of wet crimson
red
sprinkles
on my body:

my image
left
to live
in his stead.

The Compass

Place a small pencil
in a metal cage
contraption
made for circling

move the pencil
closer or far
from the little
metal point

stab the page
with gusto
be sure
of where to begin

press too hard
and the tip
of the lead
will break

before you get
the whole round
line to hold
everything inside

press just hard
enough
you will dissect
the entire world

this is to show
how one line
can keep
everything out

or in
flex the compass
into bigger angles
and draw

only you know
how to puncture
the page right
in half.

You Were You When I Was Me

Gorgeous and vile still perfect
anomaly of our wooden and ragged hearts
am I still your feral beautiful termite?

I set ten thousand traps and still
you wouldn't be caught alive
only you still won't leave my house

how are you still here, ephemera
transcendent something-other-than-everything-could
still be feeding at the hearth of my chasm

I haven't heard your voice since I ran
into the still water, it's getting dense with quick mud
the loam stills the shore with sound proof thick

vermin, pest, arising out of the mist in the dark
I know how we see each other and still
you were you when I was me

and I want the cockroach and the wasp
the clinging and the aversion of need
still the still I still I'm still, it's you, still.

I Promised I Wouldn't Cut My Hair as Long as I Loved You

I lied.
I thought that I could
love you as long as I could last
I thought that all of my dead cells
could push out of my living body
as hair and nails and sweat and dead skin
until hell froze over

but as it turns out
hell can withstand a lot more than I can
and also my body won't stop excreting
dead things, hair and nails and pheromones
and now I don't want to think of you
as one of the dead things I'm excreting

I don't know why you asked me
to grow my hair as long as I loved you
but now I'm not an emirate of cemetaries

now I want to cut my hair
I want to shave my head
I want to always be something new
and I hope that you can understand
that my baldness is a part of loving you
and in a new way every time because
I don't want to assume
one single thing about you

I want to wish you all new
to be radical bestial reborn every time

and so every time you see me shorn
please know it's my way of saying
    I want you to be brand new
to be everything we never imagined
every possibility every something we never imagined
I want you to be a bold potential and a living *yes.*

You Sing Your Arrows Against the Rock of Me

You have created a bow
you have created a gut string
which tenses the bow
you have created a bamboo needle
you have created a sharpened arrow
a rock split against rock
arrowhead
this is the thing you sling at me
you have created a way to pull back
the gut string until it is taught
beyond taut
until it is so ready to pounce
against something like a good girl
like a good girl like me
you are ready
to sing your arrow against the rock of me
at me it doesn't mean suicide
it means *kill you*
pull back the string on the arrow
you aim closely higher higher
and you pull back and you let loose
does it feel good to let loose
does it feel good to let that bamboo
feathered tip hand-made arrowhead
go straight into the body of a deer
of a boar of a wolf of a bear of a girl
of a good girl
the kind of girl you'd call a wife
does it feel good to stretch your mate
here I am

here I am struck
not bleeding out of your near-miss
it's a good thing
that good girls sometimes get out
because you couldn't hit
a target in the center to save your life.

Still Singing, Now Dark

Don't mind the mess
it's only guts and sinew
only the pale translucency
of my diaphragm
where I can't breathe
without your attention

don't mind the falling body
I left my amputated feet on the porch
where you said
    I'm just looking for ...
and never cauterized your sentence

don't mind the broken leg
we can't even limp along
I memorized the last sunset
I'd ever see from behind
my shattered windows

don't mind the dragging on
bones are litter in the wind
it's just a dead path now
a Missouri bluebird sings
from a hole in a chestnut tree
but we aren't there to hear it

it's only just nothing left.

Dead Things I Excrete

I have loved you as a way of coming up for air
even as you hold me under water
you are the gasp and burst of eyes wet on wet
you are not being submerged for a moment
but you are pushing me down the well again.

> *Well, I have let you.*

I have asked you to hold the breath of me
I have nurtured you knocking the wind
out of me by saying again
    it's okay, it's okay
I know you didn't mean it that way
I am suffocating in my forgiveness of you
choking down another weak gesture of temperance.

> *My fool's gold, I am your treasure.*

My thousand gilded dreams of some earnesty
my unearthed artifact, my private emerald
my token of total pleasure, devotion
I'm letting you get away with it
your coveting of the easy untruth
your overlooking of the obvious forgery
and it is only me I've managed to grift.

> *I have loved you as a punishment for not loving you enough.*

I have died of thirst in your downpour
we have eaten the rotten cupboard

and called it fine dining
I'm starving
we threw away fresh bread
turned aside the bounty of something new
with our skeletons a mirror reflecting hunger.

Just Cause
> (in the persona of the voice of an incipient revolution)

Look at you
done full grown, Tall Boy
still living at home?
on the one-way road
at the end of the line
of granddads all the way
back to the first stone thrown?
and you bitch and you moan
bout how *it was a dry run, man*
bout how you never did get what you were worth, man
you this lone fox at the grapes of wrath, man
dust bone, cracked sand, ground down,
hard rain washed away the trail y'all blazed with hellfire

you think you owed something you gotta earn
you think you too big to fail
you think you got power
but you bail bail bail
then be backhanded demanding
> *hey, hey listen, listen. got a dollar, got a dime?*
> *listen, got a minute, got some time?*
> *hey listen. got a spot on the wagon heading west, mom?*

just cause you mighty baby
just cause you American Steel, baby
just cause you Big Oil
you better stay mighty, baby!
you better look again
you better learn to look back again

never forget to keep looking back

look at you
done full grown, Fall Boy
you found another suckle-tit?
you still a two bit, no grit, lack wit, tittle-bit, nipple sip
need your swaddling clothes changed
since you filled your pants with shit
well ain't baby momma nursemaid wife
wipe the stain off your ass
it's all been DONE to you, baby
it's all been done TO you
it's all been done to YOU, baby

just cause you mighty baby
just cause you American steal that shit
look at you
you still suckle nipple booze nipple
bit sip chug shoot to kill
you say you a grown ass man?
what's all been done to you?

you never looked a fear in the eye like me before
you never met a bully like me before
you think you owed what you gotta earn, Tall Boy
I'm gonna undone you just cause you mighty baby

this man got tits and clit and grit and teeth
this man work hard get sharp honed
sharp 'gainst a blade bigger than you pack, you prick
it ain't *all* been done to you, baby
not like you been holding down my girls, my hand
and what you do might bout be done to you

listen
hey listen
there's a whisper in the streets
you bout to get cut

just cause you mighty, baby
don't mean my blade don't reach
maybe a real mighty baby
do stand her ground

be no wife, wipe no shit, take a clean shot
grip arm draw sling break stand
over your crybaby ass

quiver

quiver

quiver

o mighty fallen
you should be afraid

I got this violence a callin

I'm Mighty Baby
got just cause, baby

and I'm bout to throw a motherfuckin fit.

Water is a Woman

Water is a woman see how she fits
into whatever vessel you devise for her
watch her overflow
watch her evaporate away
watch her reform into the cumulous
and feel the storm of her across your plains

watch her grow green and brown
with primordial life, with algae
watch the amoeba bloom of her surface
soon she becomes murky with life
she cannot help but bear fruit
concocting children is her day job
and everything needs her

water is a woman look how she persists
corrosive and tenacious above everything
her carving the Ozark caves deep
across the southwest plateau
her body is a canyon of flood and rush
she pours herself downstream
relentless as hunger
graceful as mercy
she doesn't take the high road
she takes the path of least resistance

watch her stay low
and curving always with the hips of the land
the cliffs open to her as she angles her way home
everything between the bluffs she owns

always home to the great source
the shared genesis of life
ocean and current and womb

a woman is an ocean look how vast
she persists against the rat tooth of shore
in small swells and carousing squall
thrusting a legion of hurricanes
she cannot be moved, really
by any whim but her own

water is a woman in blue and clear
neither a dark cloud nor a silver lining
but something yearning to fall
each drop of her rain
each catapulting globe is a perfect
reflection of the entire world.

Snippets of Poems that Didn't Make It into Poems

Are you nervous to see me?
Not as nervous as I am that I might
never see you again.

I can't tell you how to wake up like this
with jingle bells in my asshole
and twerking with the birds.

The intensity of indifference.

We can always see our breath in the air here
in Toledo to stay warm we must
stand in front of the bathroom space heater
stay snuggled in bed or drive—
gasoline is cheaper than electricity here—
I say *why do we call it gas when it's a liquid*
you say *lotta things don't make sense.*

He held a gun for the first time at eleven years old.

Queers in myths, Flat Earth Becky in a hat.

Alarmingly Catholic.

Can I heal your face?

Poems to needle Mimi, they are not about knitting.

Why don't I have a spare tire?

She said *You are my oldest friend*
but I don't know how to be one
I said *People have been beating*
on us our whole lives.

Sasquatch vs. Chupacabra.
A dog that taught me loyalty
and kept me playing
a dog I got for my inner child
who protected me so many years
and we ran creeks in floods
chased armadillos out from rotting logs
and were never alone together.

Sometimes you just need an extra hour of sleep
with your head resting gently on a chest
warm, heartbeat slow, steady, going nowhere.

Wish we were all tourists
just here to see the sights.

I never met a free cow once
only jailed cows.

The grief of an uninspired kiss.

No condolences, only fishing tips.

Acknowledgements

Heart Clenches for the Grace of Folk
   —Chiron Review, nominated for a Pushcart Prize

Dear Stranger
   —South Broadway Ghost Society (#2011)

Things I Have in Common with Luke Skywalker
   —Thimble Lit Mag

Cycles of Grief Go On and On
   —As It Ought To Be Magazine

White Lies
   —Nixes Mate Review

Hearts Break All the Time
   — As It Ought To Be Magazine

The Mon Chi Chi
   — Rusty Truck

Old Dogs
   —Former People

Paper Boats
   —Trailer Park Quarterly

Break Your Head Open and Leave It Shattered on the Flood
   —South Broadway Ghost Society (#2011)

Water is a Woman
   —Winedrunk Sidewalk

Snippets of Poems that Didn't Make It Into Poems
   —Former People

Jeanette Powers is a non-binary queer artist, working class anarchist and swimmer of rivers. They can be found petting stray cats and wishing on the first star of the night wherever there are nights and cats. As long as the clouds are clear. Powers has been published widely as a poet, and *Victimless Crime* is their first novel. They ran a generative performing arts venue in Kansas City MO for six years, facilitating hundreds of live, original shows before gentrification ran the artists out and Powers became a *Dandylion Riot*. This is because the powers-that-be can pave the world and artists will endlessly crack the pavement, sending their green shoots, bright sunlight flowers and wish-worthy seeds across the gray. No one can stop dandylions. They are also the founding editor of Stubborn Mule Press and an organizer for FountainVerse: KC Small Press Poetry Festival. Follow them on IG @dandylion_riot .

also by ***Jeanette Powers***

(novel)

Victimless Crime

(poetry)

Heaven We Haven't Yet Dreamed *(split)*

Sparkle Princess vs Suicidal Phoenix

America Stabbed James T Kirk in the Arm with a #2 Pencil

Perfectly Good Muses: the collected apologies of Jeanette Powers

Dead Things I Excrete *(secret book)*

Gasconade

Don't Lose Your Head

Beautiful Earthworms & Abominable Stars *(split)*

Cosmic Lost and Found *(split)*

Novel Cliche

Tiny Chasm

Earthworms & Stars

Absolute Futility

www.ingramcontent.com/pod-product-compliance
Lightning Source LLC
Chambersburg PA
CBHW020125130526
44591CB00032B/535